But Why Vegan?

But Why Vegan?

Seeing Veganism from Beyond the Surface

How Veganism is an Integral Part of Who You Are and How Becoming Vegan Can Benefit You and All of Humanity

JR MacGregor

CAC Publishing

ISBN: 978-1-948489-23-2

JR MacGregor

Contents

This book is dedicated to those that want to be healthier than they have ever been, and at the same time, those that want to have a positive impact on the planet as a whole. Vegan Plus, which you will learn about in this book, allows you to do just that.

Preface

Veganism is not a diet, it's a lifestyle.

I've always sought to make my life and my existence in this life to be better today than it was yesterday; to live in the moment today so that I can focus on setting the foundation for a better tomorrow. I have thus been a student of the human condition and our place in this universe. As I have experienced more, I have learned that there is no good or bad, no right or wrong, no sin or virtue. The only one thing that does hold true is the inevitability of consequence. We can never escape that one force. There are many levels of consequence, I have noticed. When I act on something as an individual, I face personal consequences. When many individuals come together and act similarly, we face a collective consequence.

In the time that I have embraced veganism, and not just converted to it kicking and screaming, my good days outnumber my bad, my great days outnumber my good. That was one of the consequences. It was the opposite prior to the conversion.

Being vegan then evolves into an identity, and that is so because of a very simple reason – we are what we eat. That is such an inalienable fact that needs no offer of proof. It is self-evident. When being vegan becomes an identity. I understand that it becomes human nature to evangelize and share the experience. It's like a rehabilitated smoker trying to preach. For those who haven't reached your level of perspective, you get this feeling of wanting to shake them back into awareness, but you can't do that.

I remember one of my favorite lines in Matrix (if you haven't seen it, you need to). It's when Morpheus explains to Neo that even though all those people are still connected to the Matrix, they are so dependent on it that they are not ready to understand reality. It is like that for many things in our world, too. It is the same for those who embrace meditation, for those who understand the Universe beyond its apparent stars and planets.

Being vegan does not change your life. It is merely a tool. Change and improvement need your will to do so. If you are not desirous of change and betterment, then veganism is just a diet. However, if you want to change and better your life, then it gives you the clarity to see things as they are. You still have to make the changes. It is not the magical solution for your troubles and it is not a religious act. It is a realization that you are what you eat, and what you eat determines how you think, and how you think determines how you act, and actions have consequences.

Imagine using kerosene in your brand new SUV. It will work, but it's going to damage your engine when used over some time. That's what happens with eating food that doesn't sit well with the body. For instance, drinking milk or eating gluten. Yes, you may not show signs of disagreement, but no human being has the system to digest gluten or milk for that matter. If nothing is happening to you, it's just that you've not been paying attention.

My life's pursuit has been about making people's lives better. It has been the single most powerful driving force in my life from as far back as I can remember. Indeed, that pursuit has been the reason behind my repeated downfall in the past, and, at the same time, it has been the source of my most profound satisfaction.

In hindsight, I see that the mix of failures and successes were neither good nor bad, but were the sand, stone, and steel that laid the foundation to the understanding I have for life and my ability to share it with everyone around me; family, friends, and strangers, alike. My sometimes gut wrenching experiences allow me to understand the true essence of who we are, what we are and what our purpose is.

My joys in life allow me to contrast and they provide balance.

What started out as just one aspect of understanding the human condition and how to improve living one life at a time, has spread across numerous areas; from psychology to physiology, science to spirituality, diets to fasting, and from failure to success.

What has all this got to do with being Vegan?

The answer is simply this: You are what you eat, and how you react to food determines what you eat. If you are allergic to shellfish, your body is not going to work well when you consume it. If you are allergic to milk proteins, you're going to react to that if you consume it, even if it's not in a glass of milk, but baked into a cake.

Half the time we are allergic to something is because we, as a species, are not designed to eat it. Think about milk for instance - a cow's milk is formulated for its calf, not a human. Cows and humans do not share the same digestive biology or the metabolic chemistry.

The digestive process in cows is very different from the human digestive process. Our nutrient requirements are also different, and the milk's bioavailability of minerals and vitamins is different for cows, but we force ourselves to drink it or consume it in its many different processed forms.

As part of the foundation to reasons behind being vegan, I want to highlight a few things about this one simple, widely-used staple. I know this very well because my daughter was born (and let me tell you how much I despise this label and the stigma that seems to slither in its wake) 'lactose-intolerant'.

The term has evolved in its meaning and association, and now almost seems pejorative and lacking on the part of the person. It is as though they are sub-human or have some form of ailment or sickness. However, that's not true. Being lactose intolerant or allergic, really just means that they are healthy and that their body is not designed to take in the milk of another species. Just like it is not designed to take milk from a cat, a dog, or a pig. What makes a cow's milk any different?

The answer: Marketing, conditioning and the profit motive.

This is what happens in your body when you drink milk:

•   Even if you are not diagnosed lactose intolerant, you still do not have sufficient lactase (the enzyme that helps to digest milk). That is why you usually feel full after having milk or products heavy in dairy.

•   Milk will trigger an allergic reaction in your body to varying degrees. You may break out in full

14

eczema, or you may just have a migraine or something mild. It can be so subtle that you eventually get used to it. However, try cutting milk out and you will suddenly feel the vitality within you return.

• Milk can cause osteoporosis – but that is not what the milk lobby and dairy industry is telling you. In fact, they have done such a good job of telling you the opposite, you think that strong bones come from lots of milk because of the calcium. It does not. A Harvard study of 72,000 women showed that not only did the women increase the risk of bone fracture and hip problems; it also showed that milk had a calcium-leeching effect that reduced calcium which is already in the body. If you want calcium, try to get it from sources that have higher bio-available calcium and doesn't leech calcium from your system

• There are high quantities of hormones in milk. This is something related to the manufacturing and production requirements of milk. This goes to the issue of large-scale production in other areas as well that prompted me to turn vegan. When you need the cow to produce milk constantly, you need to inject it with hormones that make the cow's systems think that it has just delivered its calf and so needs to produce milk. The hormones include estrogen and progesterone, among others. These cows are pumped with so much of these hormones that these hormones end up seeping into the milk supply and into your body. Unfortunately, estrogen has many routes into the human system; milk is just one of them. It is concerning enough for researchers that milk is the most widespread source and contains the highest dose of estrogen compared to any of the other sources. It is also worrying that cows are injected supplemental doses of recombinant Bovine Growth Hormones that seep into the milk supply and enter human consumers as well. rBGH is not designed for human consumption and plays havoc with our systems when ingested.

•   There is a positive correlation between women with higher risk of cancer and those with high intake of dairy. This was published in a Harvard study not too long ago. On the other side of things, a British Journal of Cancer conducted a study that showed that those who were lactose intolerant and consequently did not consume dairy had a markedly reduced incidence of ovarian, lung, and breast cancer.

•   There is an increased level of dioxins in cow's milk. What is dioxin? It is a catchall phrase for the various toxins that develop or are added during the course of production. For instance, even if you do not add MSG to a particular item, the processing of the food, including the hydrogenation process or even the pasteurization process, releases the bound glutamine from its molecule chain. This results in that once harmless form of glutamine becoming free and behaving like MSG – and we know how harmful MSG is. In the case of free MSG, that's a dioxin. Like that, there are many dioxins in milk including Melamine (an ingredient found in plastic).

•   Then there are the unwanted antibiotics. Your thoughts are probably going through your mind now. Where are the antibiotics coming from? Antibiotics can't be bad for me, can they? Well, the antibiotics are coming from the large doses that are given to cows so that they don't get sick from the environment they are in or from the infections they get from the constant use of mechanical milking devices that attach to the udders. Antibiotics in constant large quantities do two things to you. First, they eventually make you immune to it, or they wipe out good and bad bacteria thereby skewing the bacteria population in your gut or in your system.

That's just milk. I have not even gotten to eggs, and chicken and cheese that is processed. We will get to all that later. Even all these issues with milk are barely scraping the surface. You will see more stuff in the upcoming chapters why being vegan does not need to just be about morality and animal treatment. We can get as incensed as we want about how the animals are treated and I respect that but do not forget to take a look at what you are feeding your body and what you are feeding your kids.

Whatever diet you choose or whatever preference of food you have, the one fundamental truth that you need to be aware of is that your body uses energy, measured in calories, and nutrition, from things like vitamins, minerals, and so on. You have to take into account what you are eating and not just the calories that are contained within it. Everything has calories, even a sheet of paper. Even if you ate something that was bad for you, it would still give you calories.

If you plan to become Vegan, do not worry about getting enough calories, or wonder if you will have the energy to get through the day. As for nutrients, there are arguments that correctly conclude that you can't get all your needed vitamins and minerals from just sticking to plant sources. Even though there is some truth to that, the naysayers have taken it to a point that has gone far beyond reason. Sure, it is true that there is a list of vitamins, like B12, that one would be hard-pressed to find in vegan ingredients. Unlike its carnivorous counterpart, where all the minerals, vitamins and proteins we need are easily sourced and conveniently consumed.

No, don't worry, you didn't purchase the wrong book. I am not here to make a case for you to stop your march towards being Vegan. Nevertheless, I am not here to prompt you along either. I am here to give you the facts as they lay. However, if my enthusiasm finds its way into my words, forgive me. It is a free world, and in a free world, we all get to exercise our free will. However, here is the rub: In a free world, where we get to exercise free will and choose everything from our leaders to our meals, the thing that separates progress from destruction is knowledge; and knowledge of Veganism and the state of our food supply is what is on offer here. The choice of what to do with that knowledge, I leave to you.

***

Introduction

There are various reasons from which one could choose to embrace veganism. The motivations that carry with it shades of morality, piety or health is important in and of itself. Nevertheless, going beyond that there is a compelling reason more relevant to the world we live in today, and I suspect, will be more relevant in the world the next generation inherits tomorrow.

It is hard to stick within the boundaries of pure veganism. Not because it is too restrictive, but if you were to adapt it to the current world we live in, the old definition of veganism no longer suffices. The original definition is simple: vegetarian + dairy free. But to keep to the spirit of veganism you would have to make the formula more inclusive. Today's definition of vegan has to be vegetarian + dairy free + gluten free + processed food free.

Veganism goes beyond just looking at whether the food we eat is meat, fish or veggies; it is more than what's in and what's out; it's more than cookbooks and lifestyles. It is about a conscious and educated look at what we need to survive and how we can go about protecting what we are and who and what we can be. Food that works with us, builds us up; on the other hand, food that works against us, albeit delicious food, breaks us down.

It looks at the nature of the food we ingest. We are, after all, what we eat. Garbage in, garbage out. Pick your phrase. It is all true. You can't expect to put toxins in your body and hope that you will be able to go by life unharmed and unchanged. It will catch up, and even though you look and feel fine today, you are going to feel its effects in time.

Beyond how you look, it is also going to affect how you feel. Let us put aside veganism, because I did say that I am not going to convince you one way or the other. So, for now, I am not going to say if you should embrace it or how you should embrace it. Nevertheless, I am going to lay out ways to make yourself healthy.

The body is an organic system that relies on extracting nutrients and calories from the surrounding environment. It uses the digestive system to extract molecular compounds that we ingest and transfer it to the blood stream that then shuttles it around the body where cells absorb whatever nutrients, water, or glucose they need. Whatever you put in it, eventually makes its way to your cells – your building blocks. If you put garbage in, then garbage becomes your building blocks. That realization, for me, was monumental.

***

Chapter 1 Judging the Book by Its Cover

Let's start by cleaning the slate here before we jump in and get all Vegan up in here. Opponents of veganism like to rely on three popular misconceptions. Before I get to them, I have to admit there is some truth to all of them, but there is also a lot of exaggeration. You'll see what I mean.

First Misconception: Vegetarians are Vegans

What's in a label? The idea is to convey something that makes you better. Getting caught up on the semantics is like mining for gold and being caught up with the silt that you have to get through to get to the gold. The vegetarian/vegan misconception does no harm, simply because it is just an issue of definition. In the interest of being thorough, however, let us agree that vegetarians primarily eat anything that is not meat or flesh of an animal; but they will consume the milk of an animal, or eggs for that matter. Vegans only consume vegetables and vegetable by products but no animal or animal by-products. That includes milk, eggs, and even leather.

Second Misconception: Vegans are Vegans because they don't want to hurt animals.

Well, there is some truth to that, but you do not have to love animals or feel empathy for them. I know people who love animals and aren't vegans, and I have friends who are indifferent towards animals, yet still embrace veganism. Yet there are those who do subscribe to certain perspectives of being vegan because they feel the injustice of the treatment of animals in the supply chain – from birth to slaughter. I can see their logic because the treatment of animals is just unacceptable in many of the farms and slaughter houses, but none of these reasons sufficiently explain why a large part of vegans are vegans today and why there is renewed momentum in cleaning up the pantry. There has been a critical reasoning behind this decision and I will get to that later in the book. Suffice to say, that it is more than that and the reasons are not all altruism based on empathy. It is also based on selfish reasons.

Third Misconception: Vegans Don't Get Sufficient Protein.

Now this one is just totally unfounded. If the misconception was insufficient nutrients, like the first one, I can buy it to a certain extent. But the fact that they call into question protein deficiency is just patently false. You will see in the upcoming chapters how there is sufficient protein in all of the food groups that are acceptable to vegans.

The key about getting what you need relies on two factors that you need to develop. The first is that you need to create an appetite for the goods that you need. When you become vegan, you need time to adapt. This adaptation process is so that your body can build a library of tastes.

Here is how it works: When you drink a glass of orange juice, your body gets a number of nutrients from it, including Vitamins A, C, D, E and K. It gives you Thiamin, Riboflavin, Niacin and so on. After a few times of drinking orange juice, your body has a good idea of what it gets, so it does one of two things. First off, anytime it want's Vitamin C, it is going to send you a feeling – an appetite. That appetite is going to get you to be in the mood for OJ. When you get an appetite for anything, there is a reason behind it, especially when your mind and palette are clean.

My main purpose of turning vegan is so that I could make the effort to ingest clean wholesome food. I certainly find some difficulty in sourcing for some of the food and getting all the nutrients I need, and I make it a habit to get a variety of leafy veggies, solid veggies, seeds, nuts, fruits so that my body builds its new database of nutrient sources. After a while, you do not need to keep a list to make sure you are getting your necessary intake, your body will tell you what to have for dinner.

The reason it is probably not working now is that you've ingested so much processed foods that they've messed with that database and that appetite system. Trust me. If you get off the processed food wagon and stay clean and vegan for about 6 months, you will start to cleanse the system and your body will know what to ask for.

***

Chapter 2 The Human Energy Equation

How do you see food? Do you see it as a source of pleasure? Or, do you see it as a social engagement? Do you see it as an elaborate affair, or do you think that it is something that is meant to keep you strong and healthy?

I pose these questions because somewhere in the last fifty years we have had divergent interests. We have gone from needing food to survive and thrive, to celebrating food for its pleasure value. That would not be too bad if the objectives were complementary, but it's not. Not only have the interests diverged, they have become counterproductive and self-defeating. There is no other way to look at it except seeing that food, and the pleasure of food, have hacked and hijacked our collective consciousness.

Believe me, I know. I used to be a foodie.

We can live our lives in one of two fundamental ways. We can live it as a slave to dopamine, or we can live it without ultimate purpose in mind. If we chose to live a dopamine-filled life, then we actually cede control to anyone and anything that can trigger our dopamine release. Bet you haven't looked at it that way, have you?

The problem with a dopamine craving life is that we get immune to dopamine rather quickly, so we need more of the same to get the same effect. It's called desensitization. It's like how you get deeper into a pack of smokes. You start with a couple of sticks a day, not too long it's half a pack. Then we leave the lites behind, and then it's a pack a day. That process of desensitization and escalation is the same with food as well. It's the same for sex, and it's the same with drugs. And the food companies know it well.

It's what many people call mind hunger. You just think you are hungry in your head because of taste pleasure, taste habit, or timing habits. You get hungry at noon, even though you don't really need to eat. You feel like having a greasy burger even though you don't really need the grease or the salt.

Every time you feel the need to eat, it is a function of nutritional requirements, energy requirements, and habitual tendencies. We have talked about nutritional and energy requirements elsewhere in the book. What we really need to talk about are those habitual tendencies of eating.

There are two kinds of habits when it comes to eating. The first is the one that is based on time. Your time for breakfast, time for lunch, dinner and supper are all functions of habits that you form over time. They are not biological in any way. In fact, you do not even need to eat three times a day. If you think you feel lightheaded or weak if you skip a meal, it is only because your mind will do all kinds of things to you to get you to fulfill such a long-seated habit. But that habit can be broken and you can adjust your meal schedules.

The second kind of habit that you have is the habit of taste. This is more of an addiction than a habit. But, this is not a food addiction; this is a taste addiction. When you get addicted to certain foods you start to release dopamine when you consume them and that just fortifies the habit. Every time you eat it, the more addicted you get and the more you eat it the more desensitized you become. Just like the case with the cigarettes, you end up having to have more just to get the same pleasure. But as you do this, you start to gain the calories.

Over time, starting from a very young age, you get the addictive tastes of the processed foods and you start to grow an affinity for it, but it's not just processed foods that cause a problem. Eating meat has its addiction too. The free glutamine in meat and nitrates in processed meats are designed to keep you coming back for more. That is just a fancy way of saying that it's meant to get you hooked, isn't it? So, I ask you this in all seriousness: How different are these multinational food companies that design food to get you hooked, compared to the corner crack dealer who gives out the first stash for free to get kids hooked? Ever think about that?

That's exactly what's going on. We are addicted to the pleasures of the food. When the food is nutritious but unappealing, we trash it. However, when they take pink slime (what they call the meat that is used to make processed meats) we love it. Strange.

I cut it all out and turned to veganism because I don't want to get caught in the addiction cycle again. My family and I went through a rough period the first three months because the brain and its addiction mechanism would kick in hard and the desire to get tacos or steaks, or burgers even – anything that had oil and salt, was almost overwhelming. But the fog cleared eventually, and when it did we could see food for what it was – nutrition and energy.

***

Chapter 3 What's the Alternative?

In all my courses, I teach people to investigate the alternative. If you want to take a vacation in Tokyo, for instance, I urge you to ask, "What's the alternative?" If you are planning to purchase a new (or used) car, I would advise you ask, "What's the alternative?" If you find a house that you like and are intent on purchasing it, I suggest you balance your enthusiasm with "What's the alternative?" This question, that should, after a while, kick in as a habit, is not designed to pour cold water on a hot enthusiasm, it's designed to test the virtues and reasons of what you are planning to do, or what you are currently doing.

So when it comes to becoming Vegan, let me ask you, - what is your alternative? In the case of diet choices, let's be frank, there really isn't a whole lot to choose from. There's the vegetarian diet, the Paleo diet, the Mediterranean diet, and perhaps we could also include something like the low carb diet, most importantly let's also look at the no-change diet.

Let's not diminish the question by confusing the simple issue of alternatives, with the politics, the philosophy or the economics of it. There is a time and a place for that, and you can be certain we will get to that. For now, the issue is the alternative. There is not much to choose from. Fad diets aside, you only have this handful, including one where you can just eat anything you feel like. The logical steps we need to compare these are not that confusing. We will just take each one and look at the evidence.

Vegetarian Diet

Vegetarian diets are pretty cool, actually. They get to eat all the vegetables and they have lots of herbs and spices that give the food tremendous flavor. If you travel as I do, you will see that vegetarian food around the world has come a long way. It has become mainstream in many places and people don't stigmatize vegetarians the way they may have thirty years ago. It's cool to be vegetarian these days and it makes a lot of sense.

Being a vegetarian just means that you remove all meat from your diet – I do not mean to state the obvious here, but just to get everyone on the same page. The thing that distinguishes vegetarians from vegans is that vegetarians can't consume dairy, which includes eggs and milk (and that includes cheese and yogurt) in addition to not consuming meat.

The philosophy behind vegetarianism is that you do not consume flesh because that may contain contaminants from the diet of the animal. In addition to that, rotten vegetables, if eaten, don't really give you a problem. They may wilt a little and may turn bad if not refrigerated for a few days, but other than that, you can leave them out and still eat them a few days later. Meat, on the other hand, needs to be constantly refrigerated or you can end up with E.Coli or Salmonella. Vegetarians that adhere to it for religious purposes also do it to spare the animals (which are considered sentient) from the misery of slaughter. We will look at that in one of the later chapters.

Paleo Diet

The Paleo Diet is a little different in philosophy than the vegetarian diet. Instead of stipulating what you can and can't eat, it's more about when you can eat and when you shouldn't. The Paleo Diet works on a very simple principle, and that is that the human body was not designed to eat three times a day. It has been genetically proven that our ancestors, during the Paleolithic period, had evolved to a point where our diet was designed by necessity. Being hunter-gatherers at the time, our ancestors were not able to hunt fast enough or gather fast enough to be able to eat every day, and when they did eat they ate quite a bit. Their bounty depended on the hunt. If the hunt came back empty, they didn't eat. So our body evolved accordingly.

Genetically we are designed to be able to have a feast and then face famine for a couple of days. For that reason, we have two very distinct metabolic pathways that the body can switch back and forth from. To put it simply, the Paleo Diet contends that we are designed to eat once every couple of days. And if not just one, the idea is to not eat three times a day, just like your ancestors didn't eat three times a day every day. It also calls for foods, that are to be in the diet, to be the ones that were available during that time. Primarily it requires that you not eat processed foods, stick to fresh foods and foods that are not processed or synthetic.

The naysayers of this diet contend because they believe the diet is incomplete and that our bodies have evolved to adapt, there by stressing the body when it doesn't need to be. They also point to the lack of nutrition.

The diet actually makes a bit of sense and it does tie in with those who fast a lot and who adhere to principles of cleansing the body as part of fasting.

Mediterranean Diet

The Mediterranean Diet revolves around the following groups of food that are naturally nutritious and food that our species has grown to adapt to over the last few millennia. We are able to convert the foods in these groups and utilize the nutrients from it effectively without the risk of adverse health issues or growing fat: Olive oil, Beans, Nuts and Seeds, Green Vegetables, Fruits, Grains, Fish

What you will find missing from this list are dairy and meat. It's not that you can't or shouldn't eat them, it is just that they are to be taken in low quantities. Personally, I have meat once a week and the closest to dairy that I get to is some cheese or yogurt to balance the gut flora. If you are wondering how you would get any satisfaction from the foods listed above, I would urge you to get comfortable with the vast array of herbs and spices to flavor your food. One of the reasons we turn to processed food is that half the equation in culinary satisfaction is the brain, which only half is nutrition and caloric intake. If you want to please the brain and get it on board, you need to be able to give things it can taste. To do that there is a list of herbs and spices should keep handy. Here is a full list you should get online or from your local grocers: Basil, Cilantro, Chives, Fennel, Garlic, Ginger, Mint, Onion, Oregano, Parsley, Rosemary, Sage, Saffron, Sea Salt, and Thyme

A number of these you can plant in your herb garden, and the rest you can keep them in a sealed kitchen bag. Together with sea salt, which is on the list, and olive oil, which is a staple for Mediterranean Diets, you can also have paprika, hot peppers, vinegar, and fruit squeeze (lemon, lime, and oranges) to give it a burst of flavor.

Low-Carb Diet

This is one of the most popular diets and has a large following. It was designed into popularity by Dr. Atkins and eventually hit the world and the minds of fans as the Atkins Diet. There were a number of spin-offs from it as time progressed. The basic principle behind the diet was to alter the metabolic pathways of the body so that the body starts utilizing its ability to shift from using food in the gut as energy to using fats stored in the body. The metabolic pathway in extracting energy from both these sources is very different. Even the byproducts are different. The crucial thing here is to stop the body from converting anything to glycogen that is stored in the liver and instead converting the fat tissue into energy. To do this, the body is first starved of carbohydrates and given a diet full of protein and fats. I don't really need to go into the full details of it because most of you already know this diet well. It was all the rage for a large amount of time across three decades.

I personally know friends who have gone on this diet and the results were nothing short of amazing to me when I witnessed them peel off the fat. I've seen people shed up to 30 pounds in a month adhering to a strict Atkins Diet, but there was something that concerned me, and it was not the fact that they were not balancing the food groups (I had lost faith in the food pyramid a long time ago – it is antiquated and based on inaccurate data and unsubstantiated conclusions). What bothered me more was the fact that the kidneys were placed under severe stress. No doubt the body is designed to cycle between periods of feast and famine, yes, that much has been proven and has formed the basis of the Paleo diet. However, a ketone spike after three to four days of the Atkins was something that I was uncomfortable with. So, as much as it looked good in the beginning with all the possible weight loss potential, I was uncomfortable with excess toxins in the meat.

Do you know what the problem with meat is? Well, since it's part of the reason I moved on from meat, I will let you in on the reasons meat didn't make the cut. The first thing is that meat is heavy in iron, obviously. That's not always a bad thing, but because it is in so much of our diets, the build-up starts to accumulate in the brain. Researchers have found that the parts of the brain that are generally damaged in patients with Alzheimer's tend to show larger than normal iron deposits in the areas that were damaged. Something to seriously think about.

That's not all. There is another reason, and it has to do with heart disease. Yes, I know you've probably heard about this and you have realized that the cholesterol in the meat is the killer. Well, yes, but that's not what I was getting at. There is, apparently, another problem that tells me we're not even remotely capable of eating meat. When meat breaks down in your stomach, sure you get all the iron and protein and stuff, but what you also get is carnitine. Carnitine produces TMAO in the gut and TMAO is linked to arteriosclerosis. Arteriosclerosis leads to a lot of other bad stuff like heart disease and stroke. I've seen what a stroke looks like. Two immediate members of my family were victims of stroke, and it was not a pretty picture.

There is so much more about the low-carb diet that eventually just moved me away from meat. Suddenly, it was not so appealing.

Eat as I Like Diet

I know this part may sound like a joke or as a sarcastic lobby at the rest of the diets, it's not. I found before I got to being vegan that the best diet you can get to is the one where you eat whatever you feel like eating. It was my attempt at passing control of my appetite back to my body so that my body would tell me what it wanted.

Think about that for a minute. Why do we have appetites? Well, we have them because it is the way our body tells us what nutrients we need. Think about it like this, when your body is dehydrated, what do you feel like doing? You feel like drinking something, especially water. You get the sensation of feeling thirsty. An appetite is the same way, your body is telling you what it needs. This is a very intricate mechanism in the body.

We talk about this at length in a later chapter but for now, the reason I like this kind of a diet is that it allows me to let my body figure out what it needs and I base what I want on that. It is a very healthy collaboration. The only thing is that I have final say over what it wants. Because I take meat, dairy and processed foods out of the equation, if my body has a craving for any of those, then I give it a pass. In time, my body learns what I will and will not allow, and it falls in line. When you get to this point, your body, mind, and spirit start to work like a well-oiled machine.

This is not really a diet. It is about getting your body back on track and then letting it do what it wants. You will find that in time, your mind falls in line and whenever you eat the food that it gives you a craving for, you will enjoy that the same dopamine rush you get from other non-vegan foods.

These are the alternatives. You get to choose how you live your life, but only one of these diets really lets you chose that life. We tend to get it wrong in most cases and invoke freedom when we make the choices we do for food. Once we make the wrong choice there, we really don't have much ability to choose the rest of our lives because we become enslaved to something that slowly erodes our health and chisels away at our happiness.

***

Chapter 4 Nutrition Economics

You are made up of three components - and this is not a religious lesson. This is fact, and we will show you on a factual basis how this relates to fasting and why you should do it, but why you are reluctant to do so.

The first component that is the most obvious to you is the body. That is what you see in the mirror every day and it is no surprise it is the part of you that you want to improve aesthetically. That's fine. But to do it well, you got to stop looking at it from the aesthetic perspective and look at it as it is. If you want a good body, one that screams success and fitness, then you need one that is healthy. Because how we judge people on their looks, it turns out is by how healthy they are - and we don't even know it.

When the body is healthy, not obese, or not too thin, the ideal weight of the person of a particular frame is an attractive quality. You don't have to be ripped if you don't want to be, but if you are at the ideal weight, there is already a certain quality of attractiveness that follows.

Our body communicates volumes to the world about who we are and how we do things. A person with a good body is a person who is disciplined, is healthy and is able to do more than a person who is out of shape. That's a fact. This does not refer to people who have large frames. This is about people who are overweight. Have you ever seen a person who is healthy be out of shape? No!

The basis of proper eating is to align your eating habits with the way your body is designed. If you're thinking that your body is designed to have three square meals - breakfast, lunch, and dinner, on a daily basis - you are mistaken. So before we get into understanding and eventually implementing Intermittent Fasting, let's take a tour of the body, a walk through evolutionary history, and see how your cardinal systems - mind, body, and soul, work together and how your eating patterns need to promote the unity, efficiency, and harmony in the three cardinal systems.

When you align your consumption patterns to the three cardinal systems, you will start to feel like a new person and you will be able to reach new heights. This life of ours is not meant to spend its time eating all day, it's designed to achieve more and advance further. We are designed to test the limits of existence and then push that envelope further. It is not designed to sit and consume every morsel of edible garbage.

It's unfortunate that the proper way of eating has come to be labeled as a method of dieting or as a subset of religion. Veganism just means that you chose to embrace vegetarian ideals and remove dairy, for me that also includes removing processed foods. Not because I am trying to adhere to some ideology, or because I am trying to convert this into a political debate. I am looking at being the healthiest I can be, and for me, I've found that that comes from being Vegan. You are free to come to your own conclusion after reading this book.

The reason we look at it as fasting and we give the word 'fasting' such a dire meaning, is the indicative of the way we view food and the way we think of eating. That perspective, and the ensuing habit, is why we are overweight and have such unhealthy systems.

The problem isn't just you. The problem is all of society, in almost every corner of the world, in every society across generation after generations. We have taken food from being the thing that nourishes us to the thing that is one of the largest killers and causes of the most amount of illnesses and suffering.

Take gastritis for example. Because the human condition is so caught up with eating on time, we have made it into such a habit that our gastric juices start coming online at the stroke of noon. It's lunch time, we have been programmed and conditioned that way, and so our body complies. Whether we need it or not, the food processing systems come online and if we don't feed it, we literally start to digest ourselves from the inside out - think ulcers, acid reflux and gastritis.

But the body is so much better than that. If you do not impose the standard of three squares a day, then your body is going to get used to it. What we need as a species is a food revolution. And, as with all revolutions, it starts with one - You!

The body has a certain built-in economic calculator. It needs to take in calories to supply energy to the body. It also needs to bring in nutrients. There is a distinct difference between energy and nutrients. If you were to dilute a cup of refined sugar in water and drink it, you would get a huge amount of calories from it, but you wouldn't get much nutrition. Nutrition includes everything your body needs to rebuild itself. For instance, it may need protein or amino acids to rebuild muscles. It may need vitamins to boost the immune system, it may need iron to replenish the hemoglobin. All these are nutrients that the body needs. The body gets these nutrients from the food it ingests.

When you bite into an apple, you are getting calories for your energy, and vitamins as your minerals. But that cup of sugar just has calories of energy. That's why we call it empty calories.

When your body goes about its day rebuilding different parts of itself, it looks at the inventory and it decides what sort of nutrients it needs. It even keeps tables of what nutrient is constantly in need and it raises the requirement. In some diets, this turns out to be a staple. So let's say if you live in a location that is high up in altitude, then your body may decide that it needs to pump up your hemoglobin count. When it pumps up your hemoglobin count, you are able to absorb more oxygen to counter against the thinner air. Athletes sometimes train in high altitude so that they can increase their oxygen absorption rate and so when they came back down to lower altitude where the oxygen levels are higher, they perform better.

Back to the high altitude adjustment of the hemoglobin levels: What happens is that the body needs to get more iron into to the body to be able to get the iron it needs in the hemoglobin. There is a special kind of iron it needs, but we won't get into that (heme vs. non-heme). What's important is that when it needs the iron, it is going to look back and it's going to place a request to your consciousness requesting more iron. The way it does that is not by actually asking for iron, instead the brain looks at its historic data and it references the foods it has eaten in the past that contained iron. Depending on the depth of the need, it may ask for different items. For me, anytime I needed iron, my body would start to crave burgers. When I used to be a foodie, I remember clearly I had a few favorite restaurants and whenever I was in the mood for beef, I'd head out to one of these places and get a huge burger. The reason I wanted to share this is that some of you may think that because I am vegan now, what happens to my iron intake? Well at first I had to adjust, but as I started to fast and take on an increasing amount of vegan dishes, my brain was able to start creating a new menu. It took about a year, but now, when I need iron, I get the craving for spinach or soybeans. A year after we embraced vegan plus, my entire family did a full medical and was given a clean bill of health. Nothing was out of the ordinary.

**

Chapter 5 Grocery Store Demographics

One of the reasons people embrace veganism is because they want to retard the demand for animal products so that the (perceived) reduced profitability gets producers to move on to another (more) profitable venture. It is working, but it can be better. In the last decade, the slaughter has decreased by 10% as more Millennials are convinced about the virtues of vegetables instead of meat.

An entire generation stands on the shoulders of the Baby Boomers who saw meat and dairy as a luxury and aimed to give their kids what they could not have. That formed the unshakeable basis of the affinity to meat in Generation X. We grew up on it. It was a staple for us and it was a badge of accomplishment. It was an economic feat to be able to have meat at the table, and as is always the case with humans, what you can't have initially, always gains value eventually.

Removing meat from the table felt like you were stepping down in class and title. Add to that, vegetables that did make it to the plate is placed off to the side and treated as an afterthought. Promoting vegetables to center-stage and increasing its portion, although cutting the price of the plate just did not make sense. There was, and still is, a sense of "I can afford it, so why can't I eat the good stuff?"

Then there are the Millennials that are coming into perspective now.

By the way, you are a Baby Boomer if you were born between 1946 and 1964. Between '64 and '79 marks you as Gen X; and after that, from '80 to '00, makes you a Millennial. These three generations make up the bulk of our society right now. As far as food and the food industry goes, almost 60% of the pie combines two very diverse generations – the Boomers and the Millennials. And the two of them have very different ways of doing and seeing things.

Compared to any other generation, Millennials boast more vegetarians and vegans among their number. Millennials are more about the cause and about what's ethically better, while Boomers are about what's healthy and what's proven to be good. Nothing says 'proven' more than a life time of consumption. So what you have is this subtle tug of war that evidence shows is shifting slowly, but steadily increasing.

When you look at the Boomer generation, just 1% are vegetarian, while among Millennials, it's 12%. The Gen X folks who come in between generationally, stand at about 4%. As such, the trend is one that is moving in the right direction. You can even see investments moving the vegan/vegetarian direction. But this part of it has me worried a little because the whole point of becoming vegan, is not just to save the animals and to treat them better, but for us to be able to put good stuff into our bodies, not highly processed ingredients that throw our body, mind, and spirit into chaos.

If you are already vegetarian, the jump to vegan hyperspace, is just a mindset away. It's all mental, isn't it? Boomer's aside, the other generations see the problems that come with eating meat and see the problems of the additives that go into processed foods and understand the effects that it has. Yes, the ethical treatment of animals is an important part of the equation. I understand the empathy and I understand the movement towards it, but that kind of stuff is lost on most of my generation – yes, I am talking to you Gen X'ers. What we need to remember is that the march to veganism benefits the world in totality and humanity in general. By eating clean, we keep our bodies sacred, and by treating other sentient species well, we keep our soul pure. Indeed, it is a winning combination.

You want to know what is really stopping you. As I said, it is mental. What is stopping you has to do with your brain. On one side of your brain – habit prevents you from stepping away from something that your body is used to. On the other hand is the knowledge that you are clinging on to, to show that meat is better. The information that supported that 'knowledge' is totally outdated and debunked. If you read it, you will agree too. So, what's left is the habit and 'addiction' to meat and the convenience of processed foods.

***

Chapter 6 Environmental Concerns

If you are an environmentalist, but you are eating meat then there is a bit of a dissonance with your outlook. Let's see if we can clear that up. It wasn't too long ago that the United Nations declared that the shift to veganism will help to retard the catastrophic climate problems we are facing. Really? Vegan and climate? If that's your reaction, then you are going to want to read this chapter.

Here are the ground rules. Being vegan is about not eating animals and their by-products – that means no eggs, no milk, and no leather. Now imagine if the world totally knocked off eating or killing other sentient beings, here is what happens.

Global Greenhouse Gasses

Yeah. Let's start with the one we all know about. This is the stuff that gets in the air all around us and acts as a thick blanket. Aside from giving us something more than oxygen to breathe, it traps the heat under it and causes the average temperature to rise. The same thing happens when you throw a blanket around yourself. It's not the blanket that is warming you up, it's the heat that is generated by your body that gets trapped under the blanket. In planetary terms, the blanket layers the atmosphere and lets sunlight through that heats the ground via radiation, which in turn heats the air over it via conduction. That heat ordinarily moves upwards and dissipates into the higher layers of atmosphere, but this blanket of polluting gasses (carbon dioxide and methane, especially) keep that warm air in. Over the years, that accumulates and the average temperature begins to rise. That change in temperature causes ice in higher elevation and higher latitudes to melt and that raises the average sea levels.

We all know where the CO_2 comes from, and stopping meat consumption can have some reduction due to the reduction in land transportation of meat from source to destination. More importantly, the part that really gets reduced is the methane component of the greenhouse gas. By the way, methane has 35 times more punch in causing global warming than the same volume of CO_2. Meat and agriculture are not the sole contributors of methane emissions though, but they are a large part of it. If most of us turned to veganism, we could move the needle and curb what's happening to our environment.

Water Consumption

Here is something that most people still do not know. The greatest threat to our ecosystem doesn't come from the air we breathe, although that is getting pretty toxic. Past legislations like the Clean Air Act made a huge impact in reversing the trend. No. What is getting us, and it's something that we need to do more about, is the shortage of potable water that is creeping up on us. We are in huge trouble with where we are going with water and one of the largest reasons that water is becoming a problem is that it is being used in the agriculture industry.

A milk cow (just one cow) drinks between 50 and 100 gallons of water per day depending on the season. To manufacture 1 gallon of milk, it takes a total of 680 gallons of water. Yes, my jaw dropped too. While we are on the topic, one pound of beef costs us 2,400 gallons of water. If you do the math, each person who embraces veganism conserves more than 200,000 gallons of water a year. For each person who turns vegan, he/she would save enough water for eight people for the rest of their lives. When you become a vegan, you will make a difference. Do you see that?

Manure

In the US alone, animal forms produce 500 million tons of manure each year. Aside from the greenhouse gasses that creates, the bacteria and pathogens from fresh manure seep into the water table and are carried downstream. In states that have regulations protecting this from happening, farmers found a loophole where they liquefy the manure and spray it into the air so that the wind carries it downwind. It has been shown that population centers downwind are affected by the inhalation of pathogens and allergens. Not a very pleasant way of living, don't you think?

Inefficient Use of Resources

When you think of meat, I urge you to think of it this way, as an alternative of understanding the economics of meat. When you consume nutrients and calories from plant sources, you use 20 times less land than when you rely on meat. That is because the vegetation that you consume as a vegan is less compared to having to feed cows or chickens. The implications of that seemingly innocuous fact are far reaching. Because of this, large areas of land area cleared to grow feed for cattle and poultry. That places demand pressure on pricing for competing for fertile soil and on grains and feed. If we wipe the slate clean, and just planted for humans, there would be more land to cultivate crops, making them more affordable. We can draw a direct line from consuming meat and for food insecurity for parts of the population.

When we switch our nutritional sources to plant based sources we can alter the entire nutrition cost model. Proponents of veganism have suggested that increased vegetation would also place pressures on land resources and on the price of food, but they are not considering the alternative technologies that are now available. Think about the development made in vertical farm technology, hydroponics, aquaponics, and aeroponics. Vertical farms can be built by converting abandoned buildings located on the outskirts of town, or in suburban centers. These vertical farms can harvest up to 40 times more produce in the same time frame without the same costs in water, manure, land, labor, and transportation.

Monetary and environmental pressures can be significantly alleviated by switching to veganism and shrinking the meat and dairy industry.

***

Chapter 7 Defensive Eating

Let's take a look at processed foods and what you need to know to avoid it. Processed foods are edible items that have been tampered with. We are really talking about chemical tampering, and in some cases, even physical tampering because some processes tend to make the naturally occurring molecules turn toxic or even carcinogenic. Physically altered foods include items that have undergone some form of processing like hydrogenation or pasteurization. Companies do this to reduce the cost of manufacturing, increase the portions, and/or stabilize the product for shipping or longer shelf lives

You should remove eight things from your diet to magnify the gains you are up for in the vegan diet. By removing these foods from your diet and being strict about it, you will clean your pallet and that will go a long way in reducing the stresses of coming off of addictive foods.

High Fructose and Corn Syrup

Processed foods usually have high levels of fructose and corn syrup. These ingredients have a low glycemic index and when consumed, these short-chain sugars enter the bloodstream rapidly and give you the sugar high. This rapid high triggers insulin production and the insulin levels in the blood rise rapidly. This is followed by a sugar crash a few hours later because the insulin gets cells to mop up the sugar in the blood stream. This repeated high-low cycle results in obesity and diabetes by converting sugars to fat and building a resistance to insulin. Processed foods have the highest quantities of added sugar that result in poor health.

High Rewards with Greater Addiction Potential

Because there is fierce competition in the market, each major food manufacturer fiercely competes for customer loyalty, market share and revenue. Their objective, and what their research is based on, is how to get the brain to deliver the highest rewards after consuming the product. The higher the reward in the brain, the higher the addiction potential. This is the reasons we sometimes want a certain fast food or a certain microwave meal or a certain snack, this is mind hunger.

Artificial Ingredients

Processed foods may look like food and may taste like food, but are just packaging and flavoring. Most of the ingredients are artificial in nature and are designed to fool the brain into thinking it's real food and that it tastes good. One of these artificial ingredients is glutamate. We all know one type of glutamate – Monosodium Glutamate (MSG). We are judicious about avoiding this. However, manufacturers know that there are other ways of introducing Glutamate into the recipe while staying legal. Glutamate influences how we perceive food and there by how we eventually get addicted to it. Highly processed foods always contain one or more of these categories of additives: preservatives, flavor enhancements, colorants, and texturants. With legislation the way it is now, there can be certain things that are in the food we buy but not necessarily listed in the ingredients.

Highly Refined Carbohydrates

Carbohydrates, on their own, are not bad, but what happens when they get refined is that they are easily digested. When something is easily digested, it loads the blood stream with carbs rapidly and that changes how we respond to it. After a meal, we can go about our day if that meal digests relatively slowly and we use the energy it provides at almost the same rate that it releases it into the bloodstream. But with refined carbs, which is the variety that is most often used with proceeds foods, the absorption is much faster and thereby has the same effect as taking in high levels of sugar.

Low Nutrient Content

Processed foods have low nutrient content and when the body doesn't get enough nutrition it translates that to a larger appetite or hunger, even if you've just eaten. The consequence of that is that you end up taking in more calories because you are not in touch with what your body's needs and you just think you are hungry. In fact, until you feed your body the nutrient and the calories it needs, it is going to feel like you're are hungry or you are lethargic. Processed foods, being low in nutrition, are not going to be able to keep you full for long, this makes you eat more, load up on calories, spend more on food shopping, and gain weight all at the same time. Natural food does not have this effect and that is the best part of this vegan plus lifestyle.

Low Fiber Content

Foods with good fiber content increase the fiber content of the gut. This does three things. First, it allows the sugar in the food to digest slowly and that controls the release of sugar into the blood. Second, it keeps the food in the stomach longer allowing you to feel full longer. Finally, it allows for better cleaning of the gut.

Lower Energy to Digest

Because of the reasons listed above, it takes the body a shorter amount of time to digest processed food and a lesser amount of energy to do it. A lesser amount of energy to digest the food means you now have excess energy that turns to fat and you will gain weight from this fact. So even if all else is equal, the faster digesting of the food will result in a higher level of excess energy. Veganism is naturally higher in fiber, because the ingestion of vegetables, beans, and nuts contain higher fiber content, and that keeps the release of energy slower and requires higher amount of energy to digest. Take for instance celery; it takes more energy to digest celery that you get from it. So each time you eat celery, you get its nutrients but you expend energy in its consumption.

High Trans Fat

This is probably the worst of the eight reasons why processed food is bad for you. It is the high content of trans fat. To be able to keep oil from turning rancid, it undergoes a process called hydrogenation. This results in hydrogenated fats and these have been proven to be bad for health. The hydrogenation process also releases the bound glutamate that naturally occurs in foods but is not unhealthy because they are bound glutamates. When the process of hydrogenation releases them, they become free glutamates and that has severe consequences. Trans fat is also responsible for bad cholesterol ratios and eventually poor cardiovascular health.

When you institute your vegan diet and you take out all these items from your food source, what you will end up feeling is fairly shaken and irritable. Just fair warning: Removing all these from your diet in one go can be difficult. I would suggest increased visits to the gym so that you retrain your body to expect dopamine satisfaction from intense workouts and for your body to start rebuilding its nutrition database. I find that intensifying my workouts accelerates the new diet's adoption rate.

***

Chapter 8 Philosophy of Life

There is a lot we talked about as far as veganism and clean food. Underlying all of it, you will find only two simple premises. If you can't bring yourself to empathize with these two points, then there is no honest need for you to embrace veganism, and you shouldn't be doing it because it's a fad. You shouldn't be dragged kicking and screaming towards something that is monumentally good for you. As the old adage correctly points out, "You can only lead a horse to water, you cannot make it drink." I am a firm believer in that, and when it came to all our kids embracing veganism, they were given the choice. Each of them chose to embrace it and have not looked back since.

My philosophy in life is simple. That is to share knowledge, but not to evangelize. Each person has his or her own path to take before the truth they find is not only found, but actually touches them deeply. When it does, it changes everything.

First Premise
The first premise that makes the logical and moral conclusion of embracing veganism is the fact that our

health is the basis of all our potential. If our body is unhealthy, what we hope to accomplish in life gets muted and relegated to the non-starter bin. Our accomplishments depend on the ability of body and clarity of mind, both of which are stunted when we feed it substandard food. Look at the obesity levels in this country and look at the eating habits that have become part of this generation. We have not been able to manage the advances in economics and the distribution of wealth very well. Instead of leaving them security, we have endowed the next generation with food related illnesses.

In good health and with a clear mind, we remove unnecessary distraction from the equation, and that allows us to be more efficient in what we do. Fortune favors those in this state.

What's the alternative?

If we choose to not pursue health for our body and clarity for our mind, then we need to brace ourselves for a life that is less than our potential. We tell mothers who are expecting not to drink alcohol and caffeine. Why? Because it will place their unborn baby on a lesser footing when he or she is born. But we don't tell the mother to stop taking the toxins that are in our food and the cocktail of drugs that are in our poultry and beef. Even fish are no longer safe these days because an increasing quantity of our fish supply comes from fish farms rather than the ocean, it is filled with antibiotics and in some cases fungicides.

To reiterate, the first premise is that our health and well-being is the basis of fulfilling our potential. As human beings are born with unlimited potential, to make any part of that potential into reality we need the vitality and strength of your body and mind, and food is a big part of that. It needs to carry the nutrition and calories we need and it needs to be free from anything that would retard or diminish our potential.

Second Premise

The second premise is that consequence is all around us. Whatever we do has consequences. When you consume something that fortifies you, you get stronger. When you consume something that weakens you, you are diminished in ability and reduce your potential. Cause and effect. There is direct correlation between cause and effect. If you believe in this, then you can see that there are two major consequences of our current food habits. The first is that we cause our bodies more harm by ingesting things that are essentially poisons. The second is that our habits of consuming mechanized food and modified foods damage the environment we live in. That damages the entire ecosystem and the consequences are widespread.

This is the basis of my philosophy of life. It is simple, but it has proven to illuminate in more ways than I could possibly describe in this short book.

***

Chapter 9 Parting Overview

This is obviously not your typical diet and recipe book. What we are trying to do is give you a sense of what you need to do to change your life and make the right choice become a part of you. We are also giving you reasons to step forward in belief. If you just look at this as a diet, it would not last too long. There are so many resources that are poured into the processed food industry that the powers that be have changed the narrative. From milk to wheat, generations have come to believe that they are healthy for you. With allergies on an explosive rise and auto-immune diseases ravaging our young and elderly alike, we have to open our eyes and have a revolution to shift our consumption habits. You can only do that if you understand what the diet is about and what the principles behind it are.

We live in a world that has mechanized, computerized, and redefined what food should be and how we should eat them. From milk to wheat to rapeseed (that's what they make canola oil from), we are slowly poisoning our bodies with destructive, toxic, carcinogenic ingredients, and we are doing it willingly. Between expert marketing employed by the big food companies, and the flush of dopamine that we are so used to from these feel-good foods, our path to destruction is all laid out.

Even the innocuous and nutritious food has changed drastically. We have genetically modified our food so that we can dictate the growth of plants to fit our schedules and quarterly profit projections. Just because the big companies are producing them it does not mean that you have to consume them. You are in charge of your body and what you eat. They have the right to sell whatever they want to. You have the right to not choose them.

I chose veganism because I want more from this life and I want to give back more. The past 25 years of my life were hard because no matter how much I pushed myself to do better, there was a lead ball attached to both my ankles. I just could not understand what it was. It wasn't till I started fasting that it hit me like a ton of bricks: all my problems were related to my food. I came to this conclusion because when I fasted I felt like a million bucks. My mind zipped forward, I made better decisions, I felt better and did better. The moment I stopped fasting, my body slowly descended back to its lethargy. The days I was back on a regular diet required additional motivation and additional push.

So what do you do? If you're like me, well, you start making lists and crossing things off. What was my alternative? As the list thinned out, I started to realize that it was the food. This was devastating because for those of you who know me, before the fast I was 71.5 inches and a robust 220 pounds and I was as happy as a fat clam.

The mindset I was in was fostered as a kid. I loved my food, I was the quintessential foodie. My wife and I were into food. I married her because she was not the kind of girl that went on a date and ordered a salad then picked on your food. I loved that about her. We'd have so much traveling and trying all kinds of new foods. Eating, food and new experiences were our thing. Which is why the thought of re-evaluating my food habits was a double whammy. So don't think I don't know how you feel. I am not own of those snobs who thinks that I am better than the rest because I eat clean. I am also not one of those who blindly scoffs down toxins and thinks that vegans are dweebs. I just realized that I needed to do something to feel good about myself.

The difficulty in turning over to veganism was not done in my belly, it was done in my head. You will be the same too, don't worry about that. It's really about separating the factors that we tend to confuse ourselves with.

We are animals that associate sophisticated sensation with primal and binary emotions. For instance, if you consume sugar, you don't feel the cascade of catastrophe that goes on in your system, all you feel is the sudden burst of energy and your body rewards you for that because that is the body's job. It rewards your higher mind with dopamine the moment you give it energy, but the problem is that the body can't recognize the toxins inside refined sugar. And so what it does is look at that white substance as heaven. Actually, it's the stuff that's going to get you hooked, and then kill you. Yup, that white stuff is going to get you to your grave sooner than you realize.

Sugar (which by definition is refined) is directly responsible for illnesses that are debilitating at best and fatal at worst. They potentially include elevated risk of heart disease(1), diabetes (7), and high blood pressure. What do you think those number in parenthesis are? Diabetes gets a seven, and heart disease gets a one. These are the numbers identifying their positions on the top ten chart of killers in America. For perspective, cancer is number two. We spend so many resources on cancer, in terms of public awareness and understanding the cancer is, for lack of a more appropriate word, bad. But we give sugar a pass.

I have become vegan because I have become more aware of my abilities when I eat healthily. I choose to be vegan not because I do not like the sweetness of my deserts or the taste of meat in my diet, but because I have chosen to get my pleasures elsewhere and hopefully live longer. Even if I don't live longer, at least the short time I have here is better lived.

I did not become vegan to get a badge, adorn an identity, or to belong to a group. I became vegan so that the discipline that would have to be made to a commitment would be there to save me the moment temptation struck.

The question is whether or not you value your life and whether or not you value the reliance your loved ones have on you. Yes, that's how serious it is. Just look at the top ten list of reasons people die in this country, and the figures are about the same around the world.

Veganism may not only bestow longevity, it will more likely improve your standard of living.

If you think it's just table sugar, think again. It isn't the only problem. Just because you don't see 'sugar' in the ingredients list doesn't mean you are safe. Sugar can come in the form of molasses, glucose, corn syrup, dextrose, maltodextrin, and maltose. And it's not just the sugar, in fact, veganism doesn't cut out sugar. But the point I took on veganism, my brand of veganism, is about eating healthy.

Our lifestyles have changed. Our food sources have changed. Our idea of enjoyment has changed, and that is a worrying trend because it is that trend that has brought us to this gastronomical quandary. You saw how milk is a problem and how our bodies are not designed to handle milk.

You also saw how gluten in wheat and other grains are not designed to be consumed by humans. When I say 'designed' I don't mean some lab concocted the heat this way, it was just what it was from the beginning of time. Gluten is the culprit and we are often mistaken by how gluten is represented. We are told that there are some of us who are intolerant to gluten, just like some are told that they are intolerant to lactose. It's not that that is intolerant, it's that none of us are supposed to consume it.

But then again, gluten is not on the typical vegan's do not eat list. So why am I talking about it here? It's because I have made a fundamental shift in my thinking about food. I am vegan plus. Maybe that's a term we could introduce into the main stream. I can't think of any other idea that forms the basis of my eating habits today except veganism.

I've looked at the Atkins program and I don't think I can survive on that for too long. The amount of meat I have to take in, or the sausages I can to take, rack up the nitrates and the chemicals that go with it. I also don't have the ability to make the sausages at home as that would just take too much work. My hydroponic farm in the basement gives me enough vegetables with the least amount of work, but having to make meat products, I think, is just going to be a bit too much.

I've also looked at the Mediterranean diet and that does seem like a lot of fun. I totally understand what the idea behind it is. I love the way it advocates natural food and how that makes me feel. I am all for it, except that the meat that you get is never really as clean or contaminant-free as you can hope it to be. And if they could even get the feeding, growing, and slaughter process cleaned up there is still the question of the actual health of the meat.

Our bodies have yet to catch up to that change and with all the evidence around us, it seems that our bodies are having a hard time adapting to the change. We don't seem to be evolving to the point that we can handle this change in the environment.

There are multiple studies and hard pieces of evidence that have started to come to light that show the definite link between processed foods and auto-immune diseases. From eczema to asthma and even MS, processed foods have been at the center of the problem. Now there are even studies that show that childhood onset of autism can be linked to processed foods that were ingested by mother before the pregnancy. That's a scary thought, but the purpose of this book is not to scare you or be an alarmist against processed foods, instead, the idea is to draw the distinction of where we are as a species – overweight and susceptible to illnesses, instead of where we could be healthy, and slender.

The Mediterranean Diet, which I have looked at extensively, is one of the best things to come along among fad diets, and it wasn't created by a doctor or it wasn't brought on by religious tenets. It is something the Greeks and the Mediterranean people have lived with for centuries. Their source of food is the Mediterranean Sea and the arid lands of the area that surround it brought them fish in abundance and herbs and salt along with fruits and nuts. But the fish and meat that you get today are not what it used to be back then.

I like the fact that meat is not part of the diet as much as society is used to eating. Meat here is allowed about once a week. I found it's just easier to quit it all together. I mean what does it say about you if you already know something is bad for you yet you relish in eating it once a week. I used to love my steaks and ribs, I miss the taste and texture of the perfectly marinated and grilled meat.

Another aspect that you've seen is that we have significantly evolved away from the need to eat meat. As a species, we relied on meat because of the nutritional value that meat had. The animal we slaughtered was left to graze in the wild and eat what it wanted to eat, and it was not subjected to toxic food and poor habitat condition. It was just part of the wild and part of the environment. Today the meat we consume is not something that comes from the wild, it is something that comes from a factory.

I used to love chicken, a key part of the Mediterranean diet. That was until I visited a commercial chicken farm. This farm had automated much of the process of growing and harvesting chickens. It had also mechanized the egg collection. The broilers are cramped together and grow to full size in 8 – 9 weeks. Compare that with regular chickens that take all but 8 months. What is so magical about the broilers as compared to natural chickens? Well for one, broilers are fed constantly throughout the day. They are given drugs to stay awake so that they can eat, and that's just the start of it. They have growth hormones and antibiotics because the closed quarters they are grown in pose significant health hazards. Without the antibacterial cocktail that they are given for their entire life, they would be dead. In fact, some of them do die, but because the cages are so packed, the dead chicken is sometimes left to rot among the chicken population and not cleaned up until the chickens are sent to the slaughter and a new batch is brought in.

Among the drugs found in random chicken feathers (a sign of what the chickens have been fed with. Just like with humans, if you analyzed a hair sample you can tell if a person has been on drugs, even if he or she quit some time back) were arsenic, DES, Prozac, antihistamine, sex hormones, and caffeine. If you are wondering why caffeine, well the reason is that they need to keep the chickens awake so that they can eat. The more they eat the faster they grow and the sooner they get to the slaughter. So then what's the Prosaic for? Well-being awake all that time, and coming off the highs of caffeine throws them into a depressive state and not willing to eat, so the Prosaic gets them back to normal.

And the antihistamines? That's for the allergies chickens get from being in such close quarters with other chickens. And the reasons just keep piling up, but who cares what those reasons are? Are those the things you want to feed your kids? Or, yourself? Not me. That's why I moved to being Vegan.

By returning to basics and eating food that has not been processed, you start to return the constituents of food that your current digestive system was built to handle. I am sure at some point in the future, maybe 10,000 years from now we may adapt and evolve to be able to process and digest heavily processed foods, but for now, our bodies aren't there yet. So while they genetically adapt to be able to make use of these highly processed ingredients, we are left to suffer the consequences, or we could go back to the balance that our bodies were designed to thrive in.

My philosophy has not been about losing weight. My philosophy has always been about feeling great and being healthy. In my case, the culprit was the higher sugar content in the juices and the refined ingredients in the pasta. When I got to be vegan, the pasta started to wane. Only because the pasta without the cheese started to taste bland and that's when I started to understand the issues with gluten even deeper. My life really did take a turn for the better when, together with veganism, I turned gluten-free.

Remember I told you how my wife and I were foodies, and becoming vegan almost killed that, but suddenly we have found a new passion. We started to experiment with making whole foods. We experimented with vegan and unprocessed foods, including gluten-free recipes. The results were amazing. Not just in rekindling a relationship, but in discovering the beauty of food in itself. Food, we found, was gorgeous by itself, without all the additives and texturizers. We both shed the weight and kept it off (the weight did add up as foodies with all those food tastings and dates over delicious food). Now we managed to find a new hobby together.

I still continued with my juice, except I took it freshly squeezed with the pulp and my pasta is now made from rice flour that we mill at home. Over the course of six months and after completely cutting out processed foods and sticking to a vegan diet, and practicing Yoga twice a week, my migraines had gone, her skin allergies that came on and off over the years completely vanished. We were energetic and we didn't even need as much sleep as we did before. No starving, no pills, no excessive running or workouts. Just a sensible diet and the will power not to give in to synthetic tastes and creative flare in the kitchen. It all came together and we made it work.

The food we prepare at home is purely homemade now. We do one of two things, we either make it ourselves or we have a supplier that gets us whole food from local growers. Even the oils, other than olive oil, we press ourselves. There are some great oil presses online that work well.

I am not going to live forever and I have no delusions of living longer just because I change my diet, but I do know that each moment I spend in the present feels great and feels whole. That's good enough for me.

For it to change you, veganism has to challenge you, and it certainly does that. The change to becoming vegan, even with the right reasons and motivation, can be tough, but facing challenges is part of what makes you better than you were the day before.

Veganism touches your soul because it starts to change you from within. By removing meat, dairy, toxins, gluten, and replacing them with whole nutrition varieties of food, you start to redefine who you are as much as you change what you are.

The change to veganism will change the composition of your mind as much as it will change the composition of your body. Those around you will see the change, you can be certain of that. You will see the change too, and you will realize that every day you see, in the mirror, a better you.

***

Conclusion

Being vegan is not like picking a diet and willing yourself to stick to it. To make such a change in your lifestyle is going to be hard, and if you choose to do it without the proper reason, it will be one of the hardest things you do and it will make you miserable. But if you do do it for all the right reasons; if you come to the decision of being vegan because it is the logical and reasonable conclusion, then you will find the motivation to do it.

This book was not intended to motivate you, it was intended to give you the reason and share with you the reasons to consider something better for your life. That would only make sense to you if you are desirous of making something of your life and taking yourself from where you are now to the summit of achievement.

There comes a time when you do all you can do to succeed and become great, but then you hit a wall and no matter what you do you can't see your way out of it. That happens when you have squeezed out every bit of efficiency you can. That's the time it should dawn on you that you need to make a change to who you are and you can't really change that till you change what you put in you.

***

Congrats, you made it to the end! I hope you enjoyed looking at Veganism from beyond the surface to see what it's really all about. If you weren't convinced before that Veganism is the way to go, I'm sure you are now! If you enjoyed this book, I would be extremely grateful if you could leave a review on Amazon. Reviews are the best way to help your fellow readers sort through the nonsense so make sure to help them out! You can leave your review HERE

www.ingramcontent.com/pod-product-compliance
Lightning Source LLC
Chambersburg PA
CBHW031132020426
42333CB00012B/349